Benny Wants to Be an Astronaut

ISBN 979-8-88851-386-6 (Paperback)
ISBN 979-8-88851-387-3 (Digital)

Covenant Books
11661 Hwy 707
Murrells Inlet, SC 29576
www.covenantbooks.com

Benny Wants to Be an Astronaut

The Benny Series

Derick Wilson

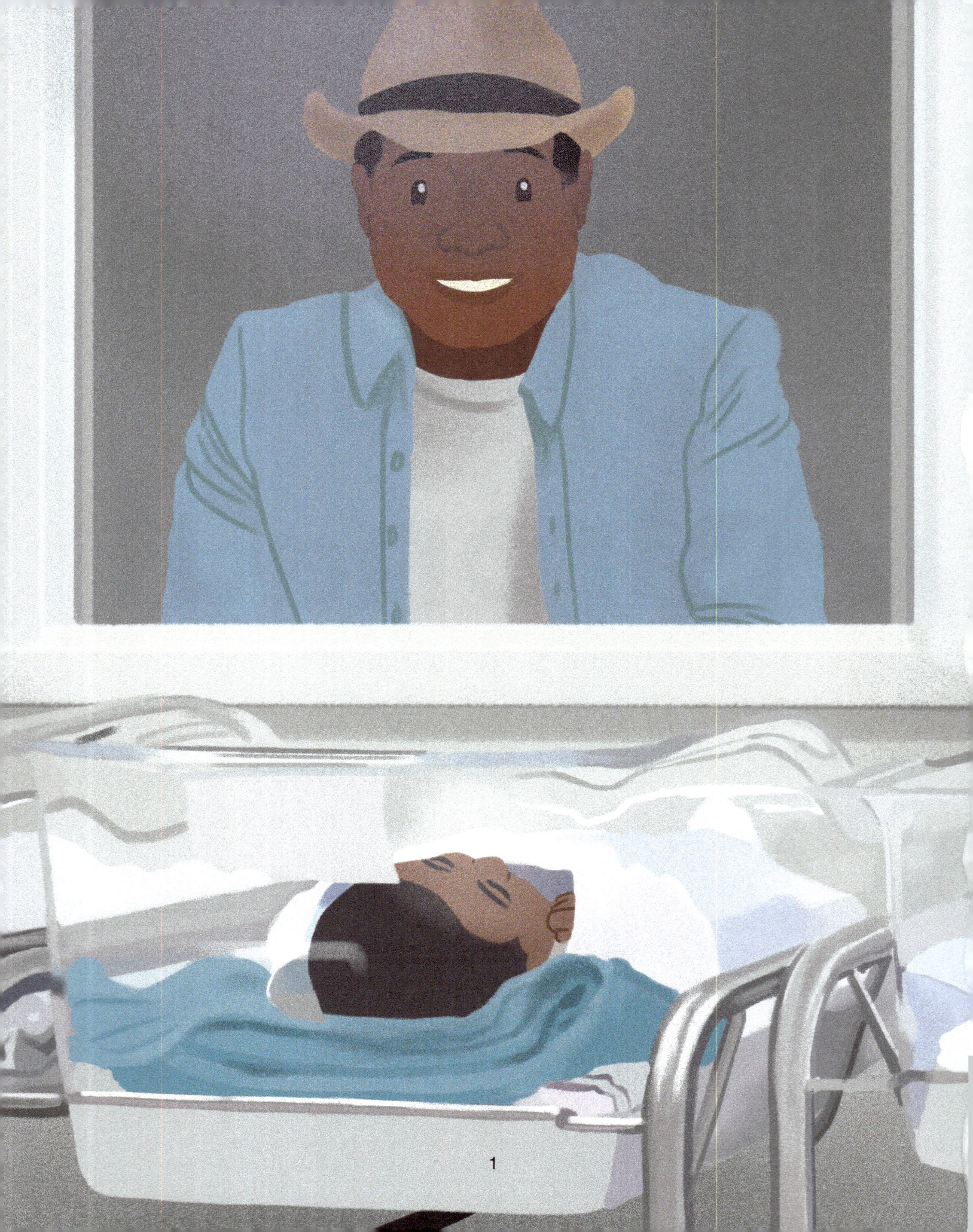

When Benny was born, his father knew he was an exceptional and gifted kid. Benny was very active and determined. Although Benny was a healthy kid, there were some things that Benny showed that made him more special than kids his age. When Benny did not like to do something, he would yell and scream for a long time. Benny would also cover his ears and become easily distracted.

His father took him to a pediatrician, who recommended that Benny get evaluated.

An appointment with a psychologist was set up, and Benny was diagnosed with autism.

His father felt like his world was flipped upside down. His father thought to himself, *How do I raise an autistic kid when I have no understanding of what autism is?*

Benny could sense his father's fear, concern, and sadness and became sad. Benny asked his dad, "What is autism?"

His dad replied, "Well, Benny, autism causes people to think differently than others. People with autism may have trouble paying attention and knowing how others feel. Remember when you didn't like something, you would yell and scream for a long time and cover your ears? That is a part of having autism."

Benny still didn't quite understand what his dad was talking about but said to his dad, "Okay."

11

Benny's father was determined to learn how to raise his son in a world that bullied people who do not look, act, or talk like them. His dad said, "Benny, you will start going to a place called Applied Behavior Analysis (ABA)."

With a confused look, Benny quickly asked his father, "What's that, Daddy?"

Knowing that it would be hard to explain, his father replied, "Benny, it is a school where some teachers will talk to you and help you."

13

Benny was interviewed and accepted into ABA therapy. To the father's understanding, ABA therapy is a type of therapy that serves as an early intervention for children diagnosed with autism and other developmental disorders. (As described by *Psychology Today*, ABA is a type of therapy frequently applied to children with autism and other developmental disorders that focuses on imparting skills in specific domains of functioning, such as social skills, communication, academic and learning skills, motor dexterity, hygiene and grooming, and more.)

On Benny's first day of class, he was terrified and told his dad he did not want to go. His dad said, "Benny, it will be okay. The teachers are here with other kids just like you, and you will have a great time. I will be waiting to pick you up when you are done for the day, and I was hoping you could tell me about your first day." Benny finally agreed to go to school.

After school was over for the day, Benny's dad was waiting to pick him up just as he promised. "How was your first day, Benny?"

19

Benny screamed in excitement. "It was awesome, Daddy! We played with toys, went to the gym, matched colors and shapes, and ate snacks."

Benny's dad laughed. "I'm sure that was your favorite activity to do there, wasn't it?"

Benny laughed too. "Yes, Daddy, and they had delicious snacks."

"Would you like to go back tomorrow?"

"Yes, Daddy," Benny quickly responded in excitement.

Benny told his dad about the friends he met and played with, Stuart and Dion. As Benny continued in ABA therapy, his dad still couldn't help but wonder how Benny would do in regular school.

"Benny!"

"Yes, Daddy?"

"Do you know what you want to be when you grow up?"

Benny stood up from playing with his blocks on the floor and said loudly and proudly, "I do, Daddy. I want to be an astronaut! I want to be an astronaut like Ms. Jessica Watkins." Benny had gone to the Kennedy Space Center with his dad for his fourth birthday and went to the aquanaut camp aboard the Royal Caribbean Cruise ship and was very excited about space.

"Benny, that is awesome, and you will be a great astronaut. It will take much studying and schooling to be like Ms. Jessica Watkins, but you can do anything you put your mind to."

"Thanks, Daddy. I know." In great Benny fashion, he said, "It sounds like a great idea!"

Benny's dad laughed. "It sure does, Benny."

When Benny started regular school, Benny had a little difficulty with some of the work. Some of the kids in his class began teasing him. They said mean things like, "Benny, how are you going to be an astronaut when you can't do this work? You will never be an astronaut!" Benny began to cry and asked the kids to stop teasing him, but the kids kept on teasing him, and Benny shut down.

Benny told his dad that the kids in his class were teasing him and that he did not want to be an astronaut anymore. His dad tried to cheer Benny up by saying, "Those kids are just jealous because you want to be something cool when you grow up." Benny was still sad.

One weekend, Benny hung out with his cousins, Chanel, Dior, Icelyin, Micah, and Mikali. He told them the kids were teasing him because he was having trouble with some schoolwork in class and did not want to be an astronaut again when he grew up. Chanel told Benny, "Don't listen to them, Benny! You are one of the most innovative people I know in the world, and you will be an awesome astronaut."

Everyone agreed and said, "Yeah, Benny, don't listen to those kids. You will be an awesome astronaut, and we will yell, 'Look at our fantastic cousin!'"

Benny smiled and said, "You know what, guys, you are so right! I won't let those kids get me down! I promise I will work hard and become an astronaut!"

Although Benny had a few more hurdles to overcome in school and life, Benny did not give up and worked very hard. Benny studied aerospace engineering like he promised his cousins and his daddy. Although kids diagnosed with autism think and do things their way, they are gifted and brilliant and can overcome anything in life, just like Benny showed everyone he could.

About the Author

Derick Wilson currently serves as an Active Guard Reserve (AGR) military police officer in the United States Army and is a graduate of Claflin University with a bachelor of science in sociology and a master of science in criminal justice from Webster University.

Derick is currently pursuing a master of art in teaching special education from Western Governors University. *Benny Wants to Be an Astronaut* would be the first book that he has published. Derick is a proud father of an amazing son, Braxton Wilson, who is autistic and contains a prodigious amount of energy. Derick has navigated through an unconventional life allowing him to expand his experiences in a plethora of fields. He is a God-fearing man who allows God to guide his path, which has led him to wanting to be an educator. The motto he lives by is, "Everyone is made uniquely. No two people learn exactly the same, but everyone should be a forever learner."

Printed in the USA
CPSIA information can be obtained
at www.ICGtesting.com
LVHW071700260424
778546LV00013B/254